MW00947684

Millionaire Mind

How to Budget

Disclaimer

No part of this eBook may be reproduced or transmitted in any form or by any means, electronic or mechanical, including photocopying, recording or by any information storage and retrieval system, without written permission from the author.

The information provided within this eBook is for general informational purposes only. While we try to keep the information up-to-date and correct, there are no representations or warranties, express or implied, about the completeness, accuracy, reliability, suitability or availability with respect to the information, products, services, or related graphics contained in this eBook for any purpose. Any use of this information is at your own risk.

The methods describe within this eBook are the author's personal thoughts. They are not intended to be a definitive set of instructions for this project. You may discover there are other methods and materials to accomplish the same end result.

The information contained within this eBook is strictly for educational purposes. If you wish to apply ideas contained in this eBook, you are taking full responsibility for your actions.

The author has made every effort to ensure the accuracy of the information within this book was correct at time of publication. The author does not assume and hereby disclaims any liability to any party for any loss, damage, or disruption caused by errors or omissions, whether such errors or omissions result from accident, negligence, or any other cause.

Table of Contents

Introduction   4

Chapter 1: Debt – Is it Good or Bad?   6

Chapter 2: Assessing your Current Situation   10

Chapter 3: Where you can Save Money   14

Chapter 4: Internet and Mobile Devices   20

Chapter 5: Efficient Energy   24

Chapter 6: Revisit your W-2 Form   27

Chapter 7: Plan for the Big Expenses   30

Chapter 8: Establishing Retirement Funds   35

Chapter 9: Starting a Savings Account   39

Chapter 10: Handling Credit Card Debt   42

Chapter 11: The Psychology of Saving   48

Chapter 12: The "Start Now" Budgeting Plan   53

Conclusion   59

Description   60

Biography   62

Introduction

Most people have dreams, small or large, they have dreams. You might wish to travel around the world, seeing ancient and historic sites. Another person may dream of owning a five-bedroom house, with matching furniture, and raising two kids. Your dreams are important to you, but life requires money.

Unless you have a steady income, savings, and a budget for how to spend that money, you will have difficulty attaining some of your dreams. You certainly will not be happy if you cannot attain all your goals.

It does not matter how old you are. Whether you are just beginning your adult life, saving up for college, or in your 60s, you need to have a budget. You need to know what your expenses are, what your income is, and what you can save to ensure you are able to pay for the bigger ticket items you want.

You could also change your desires and wants to live a minimalist lifestyle. True happiness does not come from being a millionaire. Happiness comes from accepting what you have, what you can work for, and the people around you.

If you can accept what is around you and stop being disappointed in what you don't have—you will find happiness.

Budgeting is a way to look at your lifestyle as it is and discover how to make improvements. Understanding how to budget will ensure that you can work towards some of the things you truly want.

This beginner's guide will help teach you how to stay out of debt, how to save your money, and provide you with a "start now" plan to get your monetary life on track. Use this guide to figure out what is most important to you and how to get it.

Budgeting begins with a psychological change within yourself. The first step to getting a budget and saving money—is recognizing what you do that inhibits your ability to reach what you desire. Are you the type of person to make a purchase in the now? Perhaps, you are able to wait and save, before buying a big ticket item? Most people who are looking at a book about budgeting tend to buy what they want now, instead of waiting. Others are looking for a way to extend what little money they have, by learning tricks they have not thought of.

The answers are right here at your fingertips. You will discover how to save money on expenses, as well as the psychology of waiting for what you want.

Chapter 1: Debt – Is it Good or Bad?

Debt is rarely something you can avoid. There are purchases in life that could take you decades to make, if secured loans did not exist. However, there are also debts that reflect badly on your credit report, if you miss payments. These bad debts are unsecured, and the easiest to obtain. You might be familiar with them—credit cards.

Credit card companies make it extremely appealing to take out a card, increase the credit limit, and spend money. Unfortunately, the high APRs (annual percentage rates) make credit cards highly dangerous to your monetary situation.

Taking on Debt

In life, you will probably have one or more of the following:

- Student loans

- Car loan

- Mortgage

- Medical bills

- Tax payments

- Credit cards

Tax payments may occur if you have not withheld enough taxes from your paycheck or if you run your own business. A tax bill is a bad debt to have because the government penalizes you for late payments. You may be in a cycle of paying your tax debt for more than three years, depending on how much you can allocate towards the payment each month. It is definitely not a comfortable situation.

Credit cards are a crutch. Not only can you spend more than you have a need to spend, but credit cards make it easy to do so. Once you get into the cycle of spending with a credit card, the only way to truly stop is to cut them up and never get another card.

Student loans, car loans, mortgages, and medical bills are a part of life. To have a decent career that will pay you a livable wage, you have to go to a university or college. Most employers are not going to look at you if you have not attended a trade school, college, or university.

Transportation is imperative, but do you need a vehicle? It depends on where you live. If you live in a place without a bus system or other public transportation, then you need a car, bike, or to walk. Walking cuts into the time you spend with your family and earn money, on the other hand it is healthy for you. There are pros and cons, and you have to determine if the pros of having a vehicle outweigh the $10,000 to $30,000 debt you would undertake.

Everyone needs a place to live. Do you have to gain a mortgage? No, but there are more advantages to owning a home than renting a place. These advantages will be mentioned under "planning for big expenses."

Medical expenses are also something you cannot avoid. Even with the insurance marketplace that was started a few years ago, you still have the possibility of incurring high medical debts. It is an unavoidable debt that you can plan for.

The Mindset

Budgeting requires a proper mindset. It is based on an understanding of good and bad debt. It is also based on the goals you have in mind and what will make you content in life.

Reaching true contentment is difficult. It doesn't happen overnight, but there are ways to curb your desires. There are ways to alleviate the jealousies you may feel over what other people have.

The best lesson that can be offered is to realize the more expectations and desires you have, the more disappointed you will feel when something does not go well.

The truth about suffering in life is having desires rooted in material goods and pleasures. To end your suffering, you have to stop living a materialistic life. Happiness comes from those who are in your life and the pleasures you take in simple things.

Disneyland is a good example. Disneyland costs upwards of $1500 to $2000 on a vacation special, with a family of 4 or 5. When you go to Disneyland, the temperatures are often 70 degrees Fahrenheit and higher; especially, in summer. Millions of people go to the park each day. Your visit will be standing in long lines, with people pushing around you and being impatient. You will have 2 to 10 minutes on a ride, depending on the ride, but an hour or three hours wait just to get on the ride. The heat will make you hot and irritable. Kids will be impatient and not understand why they have to wait and be bored the entire time they are waiting. They will get hungry while waiting in line. They will get crabby. At the end of the day there could be tears or disrespectful behavior. The words, "this is so boring, why can't I just get on the ride," will haunt your brain.

Of course, at the end of the trip all will be happy. Your kids have something to gloat about to their friends who have not gone to Disneyland and they will remember the fun rides, but there will always be a tinge of dissatisfaction because of the long waits. If your child was not tall enough for certain rides that will overshadow the best parts or if a ride scared them, they will remember that more than the fun.

But, if you take your child on a hike, show them a cool bone or hike a rock formation, which costs nothing—your child will remember the entire outing as fun. For some children who don't like being physical outdoors, it could be an inexpensive free concert in the park, movie, or a free market. An arts and craft fair, wool market, petting zoo, or taking them to a library or bookstore can all be free or inexpensive fun. It is the fact that you took your child out, had fun, and loved them that will matter. Just like you. If you go out and do something free, where you do not have to worry about the expense, you will remember the fun versus the worry over the cost.

If you are not suffering, then you are happy and there are certainly ways to be happy without spending hundreds of thousands of dollars.

Chapter 2: Assessing your Current Situation

Before you can correct your situation or create a budget for your current situation, you will need to assess where you are financially. Have you written down all of your income, expenses, miscellaneous expenses, and infrequent expenses? Most individuals go through their mind, a list of what needs to be paid and when. They do not actually sit down and look at their financial situation in black and white. If you have not done this, then you need to do so. There should be three categories for your list:

- Income and Additional Income

- Recurring Expenses

- Nonrecurring Expenses

Income and Additional Income

For income, you should only write down what is absolute. Yes, there is a potential that your situation could change within the year. A person could lose their job. But, for budgeting purposes, you are going to assume that your job is secure. You will want to list your gross and net income. The net income is what you receive after taxes, 401K and medical insurance deductions come out of your check.

Secondly, if there are two household incomes, list both.

If you have a part time job, make sure this income is listed, regardless of whether you pay taxes on that money or not. If you do not work each week at this secondary job, then do not count it. For example, if you babysit 4 days out of the month and know this will not change you can write it down. However, if you never know when you will have income from a secondary job, then you should not include it. This is because it will not impact your budget. The funds cannot be 100% counted on.

For self-employed individuals, it is much harder to set up a budget in the same manner as a full time career with a salary or hourly wage. Each month can be a different income. For self-employed people, you will need to use last years reported gross income to determine a budget. You might not make as much this year, as last, so after the first quarter, you will need to re-evaluate your budget. You will need to determine your first four months' average income, and plan accordingly.

Recurring Expenses

These are expenses that happen every month, every quarter, or every year. For example, electricity, water, sewer, gas, internet, phone, and TV, are usually the top recurring expenses. Student loan, mortgage, and car loan payments are also recurring.

You can split this category into two: unchanging and average expenses. Unchanging expenses are mortgages and student loans. You know each month you must pay a specific amount. It will not change. Average expenses are utility bills. Each month depends on your usage, so from month to month the bill can change a few dollars to over $100. Like changing income, you have to average the monthly bills to determine what you will payout for the year. In a month, you will budget for $100 on electricity, but the bill is $50, so that $50 extra remains in the electricity budget and when the bill becomes $150 in winter due to heating expenses, you have the extra $50 from the over-budgeting you did in a summer month.

Even groceries can be averaged per month to help you spend less on food and household items. It just takes being a little savvy in how you spend what you allocate for groceries.

Nonrecurring Expenses

These are expenses that occur throughout the year, but may not happen next year. For example, if your dishwasher broke and you replaced it last year, you won't budget for it this year. You can plan for these things, to a degree. For example, if you bought your water heater 30 years ago, chances are in a year or two, you will need money to replace it. If the roof on your home was replaced 25 years ago, with 20- year shingles you need to budget for a new roof. If your vacuum says it is good for 10 years and it has been 11 plan for a new vacuum. If you bought tires five years ago, then have the amount of tread left on the tires, checked and determine how much longer you can drive on those tires.

You can always get information for most non-recurring expenses. Colds, flus, other illnesses, and emergent situations are things you cannot plan for. You can't say, well this year a snow storm is going to cause a tree to break a window. You won't be able to say, "gosh, I'm going to have a car accident this month." While you cannot predict emergent situations and illnesses, you can still set a budget. Knowledge is very powerful.

Things that Affect Your Lifestyle

There are certain things many of us do not contemplate as we are setting up our adult lives. Yes, you plan for a certain career by gaining education to work in that industry. However, you cannot always plan for the job you gain. You might work in one field for five years, switch to a new field, or get a promotion that moves you half way across the country.

As you assess your current situation, you need to have a hard look at the cost of living in your area. You can do this by looking at websites and Forbes magazine. There are quite a few places that have started making cost of living comparisons.

You can assess where you live versus other cities and towns in the same state, as well as nationwide. It is a good idea to assess these concepts in the event that you can make your living situation better. Self-employed individuals, typically freelancers who can move around and not be in the same location to help their clients, have the option of moving to a place that offers a better cost of living for their income.

So, assess the cost of living, where you live, and determine if your career could be offering you a better salary.

Tasks for this Chapter

- Assess the cost of living in your city/town/state.

- Determine if where you live could be changed for a better budget: can you move your house for a lower mortgage? Buy versus rent to decrease monetary waste? Move to a new state for a better career and cost of living?

- Career satisfaction and income is important. You don't want to throw away a job that is providing you with enough income, but if your cost of living is too high versus your salary, a change may need to occur, including a second job.

- Write out your income, recurring and non-recurring expenses. Add the expenses up and subtract the amount from your net income. Are you in a deficit, is there savings to be made, or are you breaking even?

Chapter 3: Where you can Save Money

Assessing your current situation helps you see just how much you spend on certain expenses. It is the best way to start determining where you can save money and greatly impact your happiness in life, by reaching the goals you have set. The following are a few of the areas, where you could really save money or even make money.

Groceries and Related Expenses

By far, food expenses are one of the largest ticket items that recurs each month, so you can survive. It is also an area that everyone overlooks for cutting back. There are three areas, where you can save money on groceries and related expenses.

Eating Out

Dining out is expensive and relatively unhealthy. Most restaurants overuse salt, making it dangerous to your health. You also tend to eat more calories when you eat out. Here are some suggestions for reducing your dining out expenses:

- Share a meal with another family member. This reduces your portion size; plus, reduces the amount you pay.

- Choose restaurants with healthier options, such as a diabetic menu or gluten free menu.

- Choose 4 places, you want to eat out per month. Choose one day a week to eat at one of these places. Basically, choose your top 4 favorite restaurants or if you have 10 places you love to eat, rotate eating at these locations.

- Limit yourself to one coffee from a store per week. Buy an espresso or Keurig machine to have your coffee at home.

- Stop having coffee at noon, every day. This will remove the caffeine from your system, and help you sleep better.

- Sleep better at night by establishing a new routine. Turn off all electronics 30 minutes prior to sleep, avoid caffeine and chocolate, and read a book or meditate.

- Increase your exercise because sleeping better, getting more exercise, and not overindulging in coffee will help increase your energy, so you will cook at home.

Buying Household Items

Toilet paper, tissues, cleaning supplies, dish detergent, dishwasher soap, and laundry detergent should be an every 3 to 4-month purchase. These are items you can purchase in bulk from Sam's Club, Costco or other warehouse stores. Buying small bottles means you spend more throughout the year. Buying one tissue box versus 8 or 12 at the warehouse store is more expensive.

Cleaning supplies are the biggest waste people spend money on. What is a Clorox wipe? It is nothing more than a hardy, moist towel placed in scented bleach. A bottle of bleach, gloves, and a rag will do everything Clorox wipes will do. Water and vinegar is also a great combination for cleaning hardwood, tile, linoleum, and walls. It is a recipe of ingredients your ancestors used and it costs less than $3 to $5 a bottle for cleaning supplies that can harm the environment.

In fact, medical supplies can also be something you save on. There are numerous medicinal herbs you can raise to help heal cuts, sanitize wounds, and even eat a healthier meal. If you do buy medical supplies, then go to the Dollar Store. Did you know the acne cream sold at the Dollar Store for $1 has the same ingredients as a cheap $3 to $4 brand at Wal-Mart? Even $1 hydrocortisone is the same. An anti-itch cream has 1% hydrocortisone. The brand name for $5 that is called Hydrocortisone has 1% in it. It is the same. So don't buy into the brand name because there are things you can purchase that have the same exact ingredients and are less expensive.

It is going to take time to learn what you can and cannot purchase for less, but once you do, you can save money on household items.

Groceries

Eating healthy means eating cheaply. Yes, fruits and some vegetables can become expensive depending on where you live and where they are imported from. However, you will have fewer medical bills by eating healthy and ignoring the frozen and canned food section. People who have switched to a non-gluten diet also feel more energized

There will be certain things that are more expensive, but as stated, in the end, if the healthy food is more expensive and you have fewer medical bills, you are actually ahead of the game.

Coupons also exist. Buy a newspaper, sign up for coupon sites like All You, and take advantage of the healthy coupons. You will spend more on cake mix, cookies, and other unhealthy foods, if you use coupons. However, when and if, there are coupons for healthy foods like yogurt, you can save money. Again, it takes being savvy, finding the deals, and seeing if the coupon is really as good a deal as shopping at a different store.

Clothing

Many people spend too much on clothing. There is a cycle to retail. Unless, a pair of pants, shirt, underwear, socks, or other clothing has a hole, start getting into the retail cycle for buying items.

Yes, designer stuff is all the rage, but you can find some pretty great outfits at outlet stores for half the cost. You can even get name brands at certain outlets. In retail, clothing is always brought in ahead of the coming season. Half-way through a new season, the sales start and by the end of the season you can get clothing that is 50% or more off. By getting into the cycle of buying clothing during these sales, you can lower your clothing expenses and improve your budget.

Furthermore, if you do feel a need to buy new clothing, then start an online store. Sell your old clothing that is in good shape, so you recoup some of your expenditure on your clothing. Even if you have a garage sale and get rid of most of your clothing, you can recoup a few dollars.

Family Activities

No one wants to stay home all the time. Yes, it can be fun to play a game, have family movie night, and run around the lawn or backyard. But, there are so many things you can experience in life. You don't always want to stay home.

There are ways to enjoy family activities without killing the budget. For example, if you go to a movie, just purchase the movie tickets. Most theaters have a cup they can provide for free for water. It may not seem fun to avoid concessions, but honestly, the costs are just too high. The mark up on concessions is extremely high, so the theater can make a profit. The cost of tickets is set to cover the cost of bringing the movie to the theater. In fact, movie theaters break even on their expenses for the movie, labor, and overhead through the movie tickets. If a movie doesn't perform then the concessions usually ensures the theater can remain open.

The point is, for family activities you can save money by being smart. If you have a zoo in your hometown or close, you can pay for a membership, go to the zoo often, and take a picnic lunch versus buying a meal there.

You can also search your local listings for free events, such as music festivals, movies, rodeos, arts and crafts, wool markets, and other events. If you have children, then educating your children about these events is important, even if you find them boring. If there are any parks, campgrounds, or coupons to places, then go for the inexpensive fun.

You don't always have to spend money to have fun. Telling stories, jokes, walking, biking, and other activities can be just as fun as Disney or places like it.

Home Furnishings and Decorating

The number one rule on home furnishings and decorating is to sell your current items for as much as you can get. Make sure you are getting money for your old items, unless they are extremely dirty or damaged. If no one is willing to pay, then get the right off for donating the items.

Like with decluttering your home, you want to stick with the rule—if you bring something new in, then something else must go, preferably for a little cash.

For example, if you have decorations that you are tired of for the holidays, try to sell what you have before you buy new things.

Also shop smart. There are certain furniture stores that don't provide quality. In a year or even less that expensive item can break down or become damaged. Shop in a place that offers a good product for the value. If you do have an issue, call, use the warranty, and get it replaced. Don't let things like warranties go because they are there for any problems that arise, at least with reputable stores.

If you want to change your decorating scheme, look around, shop, and then make purchases. One store can have the same item, but for more or in some cases less than another.

Holiday Spending

Holiday spending is definitely an area where you can save. You are not being told to go to the seedy hotel on the outskirts of the projects, but to find a package that is all-inclusive and reasonable. You don't have to stay in a multimillion dollar resort, where celebrities hang out. You can choose a modest hotel and be comfortable. You can also elect to do the top most important things, versus trying to do everything and spending more than you need to.

There are packages that include a day at this park, a day at another park, and so on. One of the best ways to spend less on holidays you set up, is to ask local forums about things to do.

Don't go to TripAdvisor or Hotels.com. Instead, find a forum that is created by locals, where they talk about cool things they have done in their home town. You can find things that are inexpensive. For example, you could pay $10, walk around New York City, try ten restaurants, and get a great meal and a tour of the city. You could also pay hundreds for a tour bus, eating in high end restaurants and never have another vacation.

Research is the key to spending wisely on a holiday.

Tasks for this Chapter

- Research what you spend on the expenses listed in this chapter.

- Determine where you can save, by conducting research on how to save on certain items and holidays.

- Change your mindset to believe in the facts versus the hype of a brand name.

- Get ready to plan for these expenses with a budget.

Chapter 4: Internet and Mobile Devices

Another area you can save money on is your internet and mobile devices. It is also an area that has become one of the greatest expenses in our lives. We cannot seem to forgo the electronic world and technology now that we have it. Yet, we are also creating a dependency on it. There is a whole movement called, unplugging, where people get off the grid, away from technology, and enjoy a few weeks or the rest of their life without the "must haves" of today's era.

It is understandable that you may not be able to unplug all the time. If you have a job where you are on call over the weekends and evenings, then you can't distance yourself, but that does not mean you shouldn't save money on your expenses.

Internet

Internet companies attempt to sell you the highest megabytes per second downloading speed they can. They are in the business of making money off their service. But, you do not have to buy into the jargon. Yes, streaming TV, running multiple online shows, and computers on the internet is better with a faster speed. However, you can also unplug the kids from multiple devices and have family time.

The average household can survive on 12 Mbps downloading speeds for multiple devices. It may require a little buffering depending on the amount of electronics using the internet and whether you are on a busy IP address, with other users. However, the internet is built so that multiple people use the same IP network, which is why 12 Mbps can be enough for your regular usage.

You also have the option of bundling your services with most companies. You could bundle your mobile phone, internet and TV for a lower price than having each one individually.

Each year, you should assess your package and determine if it is working for you, if there is a new, less expensive package, and how you might be able to lower your rates.

TV

Television fits this category considering that most companies provide TV and internet. TV is also one of the main areas that people overspend on. Why spend $100 or more on TV?

CBS offers free access via computer browser. Their shows will stream anywhere from one day past the regular airing up to one week. Some shows are limited access for a week simply because of new broadcasting deals. The point is, you could train yourself to be a week behind on a favorite show and watch it the same time a new one is airing, so you don't feel left out.

ABC, NBC, and several other networks also offer free access after a certain period of time has passed. You don't have to miss out on your shows, just because you don't have cable or satellite.

Furthermore, most seasons are coming out in the summer or six months after they air on Netflix, Hulu, Amazon, or on DVD. You could wait for your shows, binge watch them, and still pay less than a steady TV payment.

SlingTV is an innovation by DISHTV. Certain channels such as HGTV, TNT, A&E, FYI and Disney are available via SlingTV. You can pay $20 to $30 a month for this option. Think about it. If you have SlingTV and free local channels, you are spending less than the typical Internet/TV package.

Now there are some cases where you may pay $50 a month for TV and internet. It is reasonable because you get most of the local and specialty channels you might want to have.

However, paying any more than $75 per month for internet and TV is too much. Things like HBO, Showtime, Starz, and other movie channels are too expensive for what you actually get. Some channels offer a new movie every week, others have changed to every two weeks, and some are a new movie each month.

You usually see the same movies on these movie channels as are streaming on Netflix, Hulu, and Amazon Prime. Additionally, they are old movies from the 80s, 90s, and early 2000s versus new. They also play them over and over and over again.

There are savings you can find by reducing your TV bill, either in a bundle or on what you are willing to pay for. Additionally, why be so stuck on TV and miss out on all the adventures you could be having? Cut your TV expenses for those holidays, amusement parks, and other family activities.

Mobile Devices

Another gimmick is the mobile phone industry. Whatever happened to picking up a phone and making a call? It turned into texting, social media, and a must have the latest phone culture! Don't get stuck in the cycle.

Unless you have major problems with your phone, such as no new updates to the software, broken screen, or software problem, don't get a new phone when your plan allows.

It is not the line cost of having multiple phones. For example, you might pay $10 for each additional line, but somehow your bill is still $200 each month. What exactly are you being charged for and is there a way to switch providers to gain better costs?

It is difficult to determine because unless you are in a city, chances are your coverage with certain providers is not worth the change.

You also have to consider if owning a tablet is really worth it. Are you using the tablet or always using your phone? Is it a "necessary" convenience to have?

For some individuals a tablet is necessary because they don't have a laptop computer. It enables them to do work or personal business while on the go. However, for most it is just another device that costs money and allows access to videos all the time.

Tasks for this Chapter

- Assess what you are paying for internet, TV, and mobile devices.

- Are there savings by switching to a new company?

- Can you save by bundling services?

- Do any of the companies you use have employment discounts? Some places like Verizon give a discount if you work at a certain location or in a certain industry, such as a nurse.

- Do you need everything that you have, i.e. tablets and phones, movie channels, etc.?

- Switch if the savings are worth it. The value of services has to be there, otherwise you get what you pay for.

Chapter 5: Efficient Energy

Another expense that many people spend a great deal on is energy to keep their house air conditioned or heated. It is an expense that we tend to feel we cannot do anything about. However, it is simply not true. There are a lot of things you can do to lower your energy bills. It takes changing your mindset and using self-discipline.

Lights and Electronics

One of the biggest areas that people waste money on regarding energy is on their lights and electronics. If you do not know how much your items draw, there are places to find out, as well as tools you can use to see how much energy you are drawing.

Certain items cannot be unplugged: fridges, stoves, washing machines, and dryers. The plugs are too inconvenient. For some houses a microwave can be difficult to unplug.

However, anything else that is easily accessible should be unplugged when it is not in use. For example, remove the plug from the outlet, not just from the device. If you have a tablet and you need to charge it, charge it and then remove the plug from the wall. A plug can draw minute energy even if it is not charging a device. While minute, it adds up.

Lights are another example. If you are not in a room or reading, then don't have every light on in the house. Have one energy efficient lamp in each room for reading or watching TV.

Unplug your TV. Even off, your TV is drawing quite a bit of energy.

If you own your home, think about installing solar panels. It is an expense at first, but the $10 to $30 bills you get all year round makes up for the installation costs.

Window Coverings

Window coverings, whether curtains or blinds are necessary. There are two things these things can do for you. The first is to reduce heat escaping in the winter. If you live in the mountains, northern states, or other cold places, then you want to have window coverings. Windows are designed to breathe a little, so air can leak in making your heater system work overtime. Leave the window coverings down, except when the sun is coming around to provide warmth. On days where the temperatures are below 30 degrees Fahrenheit, leave the window coverings down.

If you live with a lot of windows and plenty of sun, in the summer, you may find you are using a lot of air conditioning simply because you are leaving the window coverings open. There are more suggestions that can be made, but basically, find out what you can do in your home to reduce energy using window coverings.

Digital Thermostat

A digital thermostat that you can set to a specific temperature is going to reduce your expenses. You can set your home to a warmer or cooler temperature, while you are at work. Why have a constant 68 to 72 degrees Fahrenheit in your home, if you are not going to be there? Instead, turn it down to 65. An hour before you come home, have the thermostat set to increase to your ideal temperature. When you go to bed, studies have proven that a cooler room is better for sleeping. With a digital thermostat you can control your expenses and thus have a better budget for the things you do want.

Weather Stripping

Weather stripping can plug the large holes that cause air to leak into your home, whether cold or warm air. Make sure you have plugged the holes.

Wearing more or less Clothing

Why not dress for the weather and reduce your bills? You know if the weather is cold then you shouldn't go around in shorts. Dress appropriately and use blankets. Get up and walk around if you get cold. In warm weather, dress with less. There is no shame in going around the house in a comfortable bathing suit versus fully clothed, to be comfortable and save for the things you really want.

Tasks for this Chapter

- Figure out how much you spend on energy and what your current energy usage is.

- If necessary, hire someone to come in and see if there are any weak areas in your home that could be repaired or updated to lower your energy costs.

- Turn off and unplug all that you can.

- Make sure you adjust your lifestyle to accommodate the seasons.

- Get information on energy efficiency techniques and find out what others have done that you might employ.

- Spend the money on energy efficient bulbs, versus those that use more energy and have a shorter lifetime.

Chapter 6: Revisit your W-2 Form

You have a dream, a goal, correct? Perhaps you want to buy a motorcycle, taking a once in a lifetime vacation? There are ways to make this happen with an appropriate budget. A part of the method is to save on your recurring expenses. Another option is to revisit your W-2 form and make it highly favorable to you at tax time.

This is particularly helpful for anyone who has a business or works as a self-employed freelancer, and has a part-time job. Your W-2 form can ensure that you do not owe taxes at the end of the year, and instead get a refund. It is like a checks and balances system. You check that you want taxes withheld and at the end of the year, you get money back. For a lot of people, it is irritating to give the government more money than necessary, but there is one reason to do so. You have it taken out, so you are not tempted to spend that money.

The government is going to withhold a certain amount of taxes each paycheck. The amount is based on how you fill out the form. If you claim 0, then you get more taxes taken out than if you claim 1, claim children, or other deductions that you can claim. Unfortunately, you can only claim 0 if you are single or if you are not the parent claiming children. If you have children, then you have to claim them; especially, if you file a joint tax return.

IRS. gov

The IRS website is a beautiful tool. It will tell you what you may owe in taxes based on your income and deductions. The more deductions you have, the less you will need to pay in taxes. Using the website can help you budget for tax season and ensure you have enough taken out of your check.

For example, if you are self-employed, you can determine how much to send in estimated tax payments to cover your taxes. If you have two jobs, where one is a part-time position that uses a W-2, you can have more funds taken out to cover your self-employment tax.

Beyond claiming 0 or any dependents, there is a little box in the second half of the W-2 form that asks if there is an amount you want withheld from your check, as additional taxes. You can have any amount withheld.

A reason to consider this is to save up for your holiday. If you expect a refund check, then you can plan a holiday with that money. You won't earn interest on it, like in a savings account, but you also have it taken out before you even remember the money exists.

It is also a way to cover you, if your deductions are not the same from year to year. You might have a deduction for a mortgage this year, but next year you sold the home, gained equity, which is considered income, and now you owe more in taxes than usual.

Sometimes planning for taxes can save you in the end. You don't end up having to come up with a large payment or worse setting up a payment agreement, where you have to pay a certain amount each month.

Another helpful concept with assessing your W-2 is gaining peace of mind. Those who don't have to worry about possibly paying taxes will be able to sleep better throughout the year, as well as during tax season.

Tasks for this Chapter

- Assess your projected tax payment based on deductions and income.

- Determine if you have the funds to have more taxes withheld than are currently taken out of your check.

- You do have to assess where you can save in other areas and then see if you can have more withheld. If it will be too tight because you need every last penny, without having anywhere you can cut expenses, then don't change your withholding amounts.

Chapter 7: Plan for the Big Expenses

The big expenses in life need to be planned for. Whether you are looking to buy a car, home, or have children, you want to budget for these expenses before you take the plunge.

The biggest mistake many people make is jumping into an expensive purchase, without doing their due diligence. For example, if someone knew their car needed $1,000 in repairs and the expense was worth it, but they didn't have $1,000 right then— what is the best option?

    A. Is the best option taking out a loan for a new car that would eventually cost $12,000?

OR

    B. Is the best option finding a lender willing to provide $1,000 in a secured loan, using the collateral of the current car to get the repairs done?

Option B is the least expensive option. Yes, the person is hindered for a time because they need the car for work and other driving needs. However, if it is possible to get the loan for $1,000, then the person can pay it off much earlier, with the money they would have used for a new car loan.

Big expenses may come up as an emergency; however, how you handle the emergency is the difference between a possible bankruptcy and surviving through a tough financial time. If you go with your knee jerk reaction and correct the problem of "now" you could be making a financial mistake that warps your budget for years.

When it comes to the big expenses, you want to always assess the situation. Look at all possible solutions and if you can't see them have someone else examine your situation. There is nothing wrong with getting help in emergent situations, when the expense is going to be more than you can afford or should allocate to that expense.

If the expense is non-emergent, such as buying a new car because you are prepared to do so or you have saved up for a motorcycle, boat, or special trip, then you still need to conduct due diligence. You still need to research what you wish to purchase and budget for it, by saving the money.

Something that we never consider with big purchases is how we will feel when we can truly afford it.

Buyer's Remorse versus Elation

When you purchase something you cannot truly afford, you have buyer's remorse. You regret the purchase, wonder if you can take it back, and eventually settle into paying for it on a credit card. A person that waits may change their mind, find a better product, and know they have the money for the purchase. In the end they feel elation from making the purchase with the money they saved up, knowing they can afford it.

Chances are you would prefer not to feel buyer's remorse or the embarrassment that comes from returning a large ticket item because you could not afford it.

You might not feel buyer's remorse years down the road, depending on what you purchased, even if you couldn't afford it and things were tight. It depends on the situation. For example, say your parent was diagnosed with a terminal illness and they always wanted a large screen TV. You would probably regret not getting the TV because you can't afford it versus spending the money on a credit card to make their last years a little better.

As always you have to assess the situation, the need versus want, and determine if what you are buying is something you won't change your mind about in a year, two years, or three years.

What if you want to buy a motorcycle in 2016, but in 2019 when you can afford it, you have decided that a motorcycle doesn't fit your life? Then you didn't make the purchase and have the savings for something that does fit your life. Yes, you could buy it, sell it, and recoup some costs, but if you are going to sell it in six months, a year, or three without using it, then you wasted money.

Children

Children are expensive, but the rewards are well worth having children. But, you also have a responsibility to those children. You have the responsibility of providing a safe, consistent life. A life that is filled with anger and worry, particularly over money, is not going to make your children feel secure.

If at all possible, plan for children. Determine the medical expenses of the pregnancy, labor and delivery and start saving up. You should be able to get an approximation of costs. You should also start a savings account for your child before they are even born. This account is for the expenses you will face, including college.

Putting $100 in a savings account for five years can provide you with $6,000. This is a good start and it can grow with the right investments. A Roth IRA is a good savings account to set up for children because you can build it, without touching it, gaining interest, and making your money work for you. In the end, you will have money for certain child care expenses or you can save it for college.

Real Estate

After 2007 and the following years of recession, it may not seem like real estate is the best way to invest your hard earned income. But, it is simply not true. Real estate is a tangible expense. It is something you live in and gain equity from versus renting.

Renting is giving someone else money to live comfortably. You never get a return on renting. The money is just gone, poof, never to be seen again.

As you pay your mortgage, you lower it each month, and when you decide to sell your home, you recoup your losses, as well as potentially earn a tidy profit from the sale.

A mortgage is one of the best loans to have, if you need to have one. It is something that will be repaid if you sell the property and if you do not, then you have equity. Equity remains in a home, as long as the house is kept up and updated. Equity is the value your home is worth minus any mortgage you owe on it. In 30 years, your home can increase and decrease in value, but as long as it remains above the price you bought it at, you can recoup the money you spent on the home.

Ideally, you would want to take the money you make and save up, using investments, savings accounts, and Roth IRAs to grow your savings until you can buy a home without a mortgage. This is rarely an option today, with the rising housing prices.

Do your research and shop for a house within your budget and a mortgage with the best interest rate.

Tasks for this Chapter

- Make a list of your life goals: children, a house, vacations you want to take, big ticket items, etc.

- Determine the priority of this list. What matters most for you to have?

- Sit down and determine the amount of money you need to save to realize the top goal on the list. If it is a house, you generally need 20% as a down payment of the purchase price.

- Be realistic in what you can afford over a period of time. If you are adding a mortgage to your budget, can you support the monthly payment, not just the down payment?

- Are there added expenses to the big ticket item you wish to have? A house requires maintenance, cleaning, new appliances, roof, and other things over the years.

As always conduct your research, determine the real costs behind the items you wish to buy or the goals you want to reach that require money. Once you have assessed the full picture, determine realistically how long it will take based on the budget you will create, to get what you desire.

Chapter 8: Establishing Retirement Funds

When you are young, you think "I have time for all that and more." Unfortunately, the reality can set in quickly and before you know it, you are no longer 20, but 40 and without a retirement fund. We also have more temptations now than our parents and grandparents had. There are so many things we want to do, to buy, and enjoy.

However, you have responsibilities to ensure that your retirement is set up, so you don't have to worry about your old age when it arrives. You don't want to work 40 to 60 hours a week once you turn 65 or even 70. Anything you can do to prevent this, as well as make certain you can reach certain dreams after you have worked hard, then you need a retirement fund.

A Piece of Wisdom

Yes, planning is good. Yes, having a retirement account is necessary, but don't forget to live. If an affordable opportunity arrives, take advantage of it. Life is never certain, but you also shouldn't live in worry.

A couple married young. They were 20 and enjoyed 40 plus good years together. For nearly eight years, they saved, took a few trips, and prepared to be financially solvent and stable for their children. The husband died from early onset dementia at 63.

If the two did not live life, travel, and enjoy, as well as take their kids traveling and saving up, they would not have experienced any of the dreams they had. A lot of couples wait for the grand European tour until retirement, but what if?

Setting up a retirement fund and budgeting doesn't mean you won't take advantage of opportunities. You will. However, you also want to make certain you are ready for retirement expenses.

Setting up a 401K

The best way to get a retirement fund going is to have a 401K through your workplace, if it is available. The money is withdrawn from your check before taxes and placed in an account. Most companies will match a percentage of what you put into the account to help you grow the account.

It is an investment account. It will grow with the type of mutual fund you decide to put your money into. Many 401K plans will have choices that you make from the offerings they provide. It has become more popular to choose mutual funds that are geared toward the year you will be retiring. They allow for the proper mix of what will be the safest way to grow your retirement fund with fewer worries about losing your capital. If you are closer to retirement, then the money won't be placed in a volatile investment which could lose a significant sum of money. There wouldn't be enough time to recoup losses before you stop working.

The same is true if you are younger, the investment you choose may take more risks knowing that you have time for the ups and downs of the stock market to be replaced. If you had investments during the latest recession and didn't panic, you may have come out ahead or at least broke even. True you lost on the investment in the short term, but stayed the course and made back the losses and probably gained more profit. The reason for this is that you didn't have to try to plan when to re-buy into the market. It can be tricky to know when the best time to purchase stocks and bonds again after such a long recession.

If you don't want to use your companies 401K or they don't offer one, then you need to invest on your own. There are many companies out there that can help you with this. Fidelity, Charles Schwab and Edward Jones are just some of the names you may be familiar with. They have representatives that can look at your finances and your retirement goals and suggest where to place your money. They will manage it for you and you can make changes when you decide to do so. The thing to watch out for with this type of investment idea are the fees associated with some of the funds. Certain ones can carry incredibly high fees which defeats the purpose of saving. Your financial manager or financial planner will address these options with you.

If you want to try to do it yourself there are several places that you can train online. For a fee, you can take the various levels of training and then practice with a paper account until you are ready to invest with your own money. Hands on types may feel this is the best fit for them. If you are a person that needs to have control over your investments, then this could be a viable option for you.

Once you have decided on which method you are going to use for your retirement, implement it as soon as you are able. A good rule to follow is to pay yourself first and then everyone else. While this may seem impossible, even a small amount put away for emergencies and retirement can grow into a sizable sum. Generally, the experts say to take out 15% of each paycheck, more if you are in your early 20's or 30's and put it to work making you more money. If this is too steep an amount to start with do 5%. You can always find small ways to limit spending and put 5% into retirement.

If you are paid twice a month, earn $13.00 an hour and are paid twice a month the investment of $52.00 per paycheck is 5% of your gross income. Look at your expenses and see where you can cut down. You might cut down on that specialty coffee every day or eating lunch out a few times a week. Once you become budget minded, you will find ways to save and get excited about it, too.

Tasks for this Chapter

- Choose a retirement fund option: 401K, stock market investing, or another option.

- Budget the best percentage for your retirement fund, 5% or higher.

- If you start out low, and have debts to pay down, then get your debts paid quickly and allocate that savings towards your retirement.

When choosing an investment option, make sure you are comfortable with it. Don't just go with what your financial advisor suggests. They are experts, but if you are going to worry about losses, then it is not going to do you any good to invest in high risk-high reward stocks, bonds, or mutual funds.

Chapter 9: Starting a Savings Account

A savings account is different than your retirement fund. You may still wish to use a Roth IRA style of account. Roth IRAs tend to have higher interest rates, but there are also penalties associated with early release of the funds. A Roth IRA is better, if you know in a certain time period you will not be accessing those funds.

You might wish to have a regular savings account and also a Roth IRA. In this way, you pay into an account that will grow faster with interest, as well as requiring a certain amount paid in each month. It keeps you regular about saving money, without having instant access.

A savings account at your local bank should be used as an emergency and fun fund. This is the account you will place any money you have left over after you pay your expenses, taxes, and into your retirement accounts.

It is the money you are saving for some of those big ticket items like a motorcycle, new TV, or emergency needs such as a sudden car breakdown, tire blow out or other emergency expense.

The Rules

- You should have six months of expenses and mortgage money in your savings account. In the event that you lose your job or become ill, this money can make the payments for you.

- Experts state someone in their 20s or 30s should be putting 20% of their income in savings accounts. This includes retirement funds. Ideally, you will break 20% of your income into retirement, Roth IRA, and savings.

The first rule is fairly obvious. You want to be protected in the event the unthinkable happens and you lose your job or are on disability for a little while. You can move through your savings pretty fast if it is only enough to cover a month or two.

The second rule is less obvious—it hinges on financial analysts. Financial analysts have done extensive studies regarding financial independence, debt, and secure retirements. These individuals arrived at a conclusion. You need to save 20% of your income in you are in your 20s and 30s because you have enough time to gain financial independence before you are too old to enjoy it.

It is understandably difficult to make this happen. Emergencies crop up out of nowhere. Suddenly an unplanned event happens like a death, marriage, or child and you need the money you were trying to save.

Most Americans today struggle with getting savings set up because life makes it difficult. They don't have a high paying job or an emergency happens. One spouse loses a job or another person doesn't have two incomes, but neither do they make a livable income. There are ways to fix these problems. You have to be willing to make some very tough cuts, to fit your current income versus the life you wish to live.

Those who make money work hard, remain strong, and rise in the face of adversity. They do not let things get them down and they are not afraid of taking a second job, just because it is not a glamorous position. While working extra shifts or taking a second job isn't ideal, but it doesn't have to be a long term proposition if you save your money wisely. Getting ahead by working more for a year or two could see you having a great retirement as well as a happy life in the meantime.

Budgeting can be a lifestyle rather than a punishment. Don't think of it as a bad thing, but as a way to incorporate more joy and happiness in your life. Saving for that special vacation or affordable home should be something to look forward to and getting there a quest not drudgery. If you can change your mindset as well as your budgeting process life can be wonderful. The burden of not having enough to live on now or in the future will be lifted.

Tasks for this Chapter

- Shop around for the best savings account. It may not be the bank you have your checking account with. Many of the internet banks or small banks have been swallowed by the larger banks due to the financial crisis, but if you look hard enough, you might find a bank willing to offer a better savings account than your own.

- Your savings account needs to provide you with the highest interest rate offered in today's market. It won't be very much, maybe not even more than 1%, but it is still earnings on your invested money.

- Choose a savings account that does not give you easy access. If you can make a transfer from your savings to your checking with a few clicks of the mouse—it is too accessible. You will be tempted to touch that money, even if it is not an emergency.

- Make sure if you are saving 5% or more in a retirement account that you are at least putting 20% of your entire income into a savings account. It might take a little time to work up to 20% because of credit card debt, but trust in the truth—you won't miss the money if it is automatically removed from your view each month. You'll barely remember that it was part of your income.

- When you do get a savings account, ask for your employer to divide your check. Put the money you want to save directly into your new savings account and have the rest of your net income deposited into your checking. In this way, you won't have to think about transferring the money. It just goes there. It is an out of sight, out of mind concept.

Chapter 10: Handling Credit Card Debt

Credit card debt, if you already have some, is the first thing you need to handle in order to establish a decent budget. Credit cards provide you a way to pay for goods, but it is rare that you can find an APR below 15% nowadays. If you do not pay off your credit card each month, then you end up paying more for the goods you purchased due to the interest rate you are charged.

It is a difficult cycle to end. You don't want to suffer from credit card debt. It is far better to adopt a mindset that says, "if I can't pay for it, then I don't need it." You will get a few tips on changing your mindset and the steps for improvement, soon.

For now, let's assess what you should and should not do with credit cards.

How to use a Credit Card

If you feel insecure without a backup emergency plan, then take out a credit card. This credit card needs to be placed in a safe for emergency purposes or in a different area of your wallet or purse. You never want your credit card to be next to your cash and debit card. You basically want to forget about having the card. If you see it and are reminded that you have it, then it is easier for you to consider using it for big ticket purchases that you should be saving up for.

There is one more way that you can use a credit card; however, it takes a very self-disciplined individual to use the credit card this way. Most people do not have the self-control to use it in the manner about to be described.

- You get a credit card for the rewards it provides, such as 1% cash back, air miles, gas rewards, etc.

- You use the card for groceries, gas, airline tickets, and other purchases.

- However, when using the card for purchases, you go home and pay the exact amount you just spent with the card.

- You will not let your credit card carry a balance, even for a day.

It is true that if you pay your card in the same month that you put the charges on the card, you will not be charged the interest rate. It is only when the card carries over to a new month. However, leaving the amount on there for the entire month and then paying it off can lead to trouble.

You are tempted to spend the money you have in your checking account on other items versus paying off the card. If you are going to use a card for rewards, then you must pay the amount off right away. You will know exactly what you spent in a day as long as you keep the receipts.

You also have technology that makes it possible for you to pay the correct amount to your credit card from anywhere you are currently located.

There is one rule to this usage that you must always follow:

Never use it to spend money you do not have, but will have!

Most people are paid biweekly. You know exactly when your money is coming in, but if you are spending money, you do not yet have, then you could start on a debt cycle you are unable to get out of. You will justify waiting to make a payment to your credit card. You'll start to say, "when I get paid, I'll pay this off." You should only ever spend what you have on a credit card, if you want to make rewards.

The rewards are great, but for most people they start the credit card debt cycle that is never ending. So rather than get into that situation, don't have credit cards. Ignore the rewards and pay for what you can afford. If you follow the method of ignoring credit cards, then you will never be tempted to overspend.

Paying off Credit Cards

Studies have shown that the average American has at least three credit cards in their wallet. Worse, these three credit cards have at least half of the credit limit spent. These same Americans do not have the savings to pay off the debt. They can only pay the minimum payment, which means 30 years later they may pay the debt off—that is if they do not add to it.

There are steps for handing credit card debt. They start with understanding your income, expenses, and finding any savings and leftover money in the month. You will learn more about a "start now" budget process, but for now here are the steps for getting rid of your credit card debt.

- Determine how much money you have to pay towards your credit card debt.

- Calculate your net income.

- Allocate funds to utilities, TV, internet, mobile devices, groceries, fuel, and other monthly expenses. Do not include the credit card monthly minimum payments.

- Call your credit card company or companies. Determine if any credit card you currently have, has a 0% balance transfer deal.

- Ask the credit card company what percentage they charge for the transfer. This transfer fee is usually 3%, but it can be higher.

- If no credit card company that you have your credit cards through is offering a balance transfer deal, determine if your credit is in good standing and shop around for a balance transfer deal with another company. Only take out this new credit card if they can approve you for your entire credit card debt. If you cannot obtain a credit limit that matches the debt you have, then do not open a new card. It is not worth opening a new card unless you can consolidate all of your credit card debt to one card with a 0% APR.

- If the 0% deal is not possible, assess your current situation. Ask your credit companies if they are at least willing to reduce your APR. Most will not, unless you are in good standing and have never had any credit problems like collections or bankruptcy.

- Whether the credit card companies are willing to lower your APR or not, you will want to choose the card with the highest APR to pay off first.

Additionally, you will want to see about transferring a balance and whether the 3% fee is negligible based on the savings. For example, if you have three cards:

1. 12% APR with 50% of the credit limit available

2. 20% APR with 25% of the credit limit available

3. 23% APR with 75% of the credit limit available

You might find that transferring the amount you have on the card three to the 12% APR credit card, actually saves you money in the end, despite the 3% fee. However, it may not. The point is, calculate the costs you will have to pay for the transfer versus what you will pay out in interest until that amount is paid off. You know that 12% is less than 23%, plus the 3% fee is a onetime fee rather than a continuous 3% each month. Overall, the savings may be worth the transfer.

You won't know until you make calculations. If you can get one card gone, then you only have to worry about two. Of course, there has to be enough on one card to make the full transfer or at least enough of a transfer that you can pay off the third credit card in a month or two.

Ideally, you want to consolidate all cards into one. It may not be possible, so always start with the highest interest rate. Get this one gone by paying the minimum balance to your other cards. Pay all extra money to your highest interest rate credit card, until it is paid off.

After one card is paid off, go to the next highest APR credit card. You are now paying the minimum to that card, plus everything you paid to the first card you paid off.

By the time you get to your last credit card, you are making a higher payment because you are paying the minimum payment from the other cards, plus the extra money you have during the month.

As soon as you get that last credit card paid off, you have all of that money you were paying out in a month to put towards your savings or a special vacation.

Unfortunately, it can take quite a while to get everything paid down, depending on how high your balances are and what you are able to pay towards these cards for the month.

A Final Word

You still need to pay a portion of your income into a savings account, whether it is easily accessible or a retirement account. Even, if you are only putting away 5% of your income in savings, you are at least planning for an emergency.

A lot of the time credit card consumers put all their money into paying off their card, then have to turn around and use the card in an emergency because they do not have any savings. You don't want to use your card as you are paying it down or after you have paid it off.

Additionally, you need to cut up each credit card and close the account the minute you have paid it off. You don't want to leave temptation lying around.

This chapter will not have a tasks section because you have been given the outline of what to do. It is time to start now, in figuring out how to pay off those credit card debts.

Chapter 11: The Psychology of Saving

A little about the mindset you have, has been discussed, but now it is time to truly determine the things you can do to improve the psychology of your spending. These will help as you analyze the "start now" budgeting plan.

Your Upbringing

How we are raised can in part determine how we spend money now. Psychological concerns and stress can lead some individuals to spend money incorrectly.

A young woman was raised without her family having a lot of money. She was also the last of 5 children. She had hand-me-downs, no eating out, and no toys that were truly her own. When she grew up, she was very stressed whenever she did not have enough money to pay for items. In fact, she would go out on spending sprees buying clothing and other items because she "deserved" to have a little fun and live a life, even though she could not afford it. She was "tired of not being able to enjoy life," even after working so hard for the little income she could make. She knew she should not spend the money, but she could not stop herself.

This young woman's husband would put a cushion in her account. He would put $500 in the account, but not let her see the bank statements or record it in her checking account register. She was always safe to spend money, and was told to spend some money on herself, and she would. Occasionally, she would overspend, but there was the cushion in her account.

You can have parents that provide you with many things, but teach you responsible spending, and you can still overspend your income. You can also have parents who spend and spend, buying you whatever you want, and you figure you can do the same because you weren't taught responsibility.

If you can understand the psychology behind your spending habits from your upbringing, then you can start to change your mindset.

How do you spend your income now?

You have to be very analytical and truthful when you assess how you spend. You will write down what you make and what you spend. This will help you see the black and white of it all, but you also need to go deeper now.

If you overspent last month, why did you do so? Were you overly stressed? Did you feel tired that you could not buy what you wanted? Were you frustrated? Did you think you had the money to spend, but did not sit down to analyze your budget and all that needed to be paid? Did you forget about a bill?

Analyzing your current spending habits, along with the emotions you are feeling will help you determine what you need to do to correct your mindset.

How do you want to spend your money?

What is your ideal situation, with the money you are making now? What are your goals? What do you hope for later in life, as well as when you reach retirement? Are these goals materialistic or are they something that will truly make you happy to the point that you can keep to your budget?

What will make you stick to your budget?

Tasks for Changing your Mindset

Once you have assessed your upbringing, current spending habits, and how you wish to spend your money in the future, you are ready to follow the tasks outlined here:

- Write your short-term goals on a poster board.

- List the short-term goals by cost and importance.

- Write down your long-term goals.

- List these goals by cost, importance, and the reasonable date of reaching that goal.

- Assess the list, are there things you don't really need or truly want, but think you would like to have? Sometimes we want something because we see it and it sounds great, but after thinking about it, we know it will sit and gather dust for 75% of the time. Motorcycles, gaming consoles, and other products tend to sit more often than they are used because of our busy lives.

- Remove anything that you do not think you will have time to truly enjoy.

- Now assess your list goals again, determine if you want to re-order anything in order of importance. Do so if it needs to be changed, otherwise, you are now ready to post this board somewhere you will see it. You want to look at this board each day. Take a picture so it is in your phone too.

- When you go shopping, pull out your phone, look at the short and long term goals you have. Is there something in your cart that you can forgo buying in order to save up for the true goals you have? For example, if you are buying brownie mix that is $2.50 is it more important to you than one of your short or long term goals?

Yes, $2.50 is not much, but what if you pick that product up each time you go shopping? Let's say it is a latte for $2.50 and you get one each week. You are spending $145 each year for one latte a week. Imagine if you are buying a latte for $2.50 on a daily basis! It is $912.50 for a latte at $2.50 for 365 days. Now let's use reality. Most tall lattes at Starbucks are about $4, and you probably leave $1 tip. If you did this each day, then 5 times 365 equals $1825. You could be spending that much on your coffee. Let's say you don't get coffee every day, but sometimes you spend $5 on lunch, so it still equals $1825.

What could you do with $1825? You could go to Disney. You could visit Europe, Canada, go on a Caribbean Cruise or buy a used motorcycle.

You can see from simply determining what you are spending and assessing your true goals, how you can begin to change your mindset.

A dose of reality is often the best way for you to limit how much you spend on items in the now versus saving up for the things you truly want. Yes, it is nice to spend money on something you want like a new blouse because it makes you look great, but need versus want is what truly determines if you reach your ultimate life goals.

Tasks for this Chapter

- Set your goals

- Take a picture of those goals or have them in your wallet

- Look at your goals every time you want to buy something you want versus need

- Take a breath or ten breaths

- Analyze your emotions, your stress level, and why you feel you must have it

- Use meditation at home to release your stress and feelings of "deserving" something special

- Reevaluate your emotions and your desires to spend money now versus on your goals later on

Chapter 12: The "Start Now" Budgeting Plan

You have reached the budgeting plan that you can start now. You have been through this book doing the tasks at the end of each chapter. Now it is time to determine the best way to get those goals you have set.

1. Take your current income.

2. Collect your receipts.

3. Organize your receipts into categories: utility bills, mortgage, dining out, household and groceries, personal expenses (clothing), fuel, phone, TV, internet, and other monthly expenses you might have.

4. Add up each category to see what you have spent for the year, so far or take last year's receipts and do the same.

5. Now add up all the expenses.

6. Subtract the expenses from your income.

7. What is the number? Do you have a negative number? Is it a positive number? Write that number down.

8. In what categories of expenses can you save? If you need to go through your where to save money tasks and determine where you can save.

9. Call the companies and reduce your expenses, ask for any loyalty customer deals, and reduce as many of your expenses as possible regarding bills you have.

10. For groceries, fuel, and other expenses that change, determine what you can eliminate to save money. What foods are not necessities? Is there a way to save fuel based on how you drive, where you go, and how many stops you make? Adjust your life to focus on what you want more versus what you want now.

11. Reduce eating out to 1 time a week. Spend more on healthy foods at the grocery store, including items you will take for lunches.

12. Go to a bank and open a savings account with $50 to $100, whatever their minimum requirement is. You are actively saving now.

13. At work, ask to fill out a new W-2 form.

14. If you have a 401K, start tracking it on a weekly basis. Make adjustments to your investment if you are not seeing a decent return. Speak with an advisor if you feel you need advice.

15. Speak with a financial advisor anyway. A financial advisor can assess your spending, living expenses, and retirement accounts and make adjustments you might not have thought about. There are free services and for a while places like Fidelity will be able to offer you advice without a fee. This free banking advice may change if certain votes are passed.

16. Make an extra credit card payment, even if it is only $5. It might seem silly, but making an extra $5 payment, right now, will bolster your confidence and make you feel as though you have accomplished something towards your budget and debts.

17. Look at vacation packages. You do not have to buy, but simply research, set up alerts for better pricing, and make you feel as if you are going to be able to go. However, as you do this, make sure you are entering reasonable dates.

If your budget, even with new savings, will not allow for a vacation this year, then look at the dates when you know you can.

18. If your goal is to buy a new car, home, motorcycle or other big ticket item, start researching what you want. How much does it cost? What are long term costs? How long is the product life? Where can you buy this item? Following through on research helps you feel an accomplishment towards that goal, even if you cannot reach that goal for another year, two years, or five years.

19. Today, do not buy one thing that is desired. Forgo the coffee from Starbucks, don't eat out, or don't buy something unhealthy from the grocery store. Cut out one thing for your daily routine that is desired, not needed.

20. Remember that your suffering and overspending, usually comes from a lack of happiness within.

The Envelope Method

This is also a "start now" plan you can follow through with today.

1. Go to the ATM.

2. Remove the money you need for expenses, all expenses, unless you are going to make a payment today or in three days via ACH.

3. Put that money in envelopes marked for the expense: TV, internet, phone, gas, groceries, household, etc.

4. Leave the money in the envelope until you need it.

5. Use cash for gas, groceries, household items, and all expenses that you cannot pay via ACH payments.

6. When an ACH payment is approaching put the money back in the checking account, set up the payment, and pay

the bill all within 48 hours. If the bill is automatic each month, just put the money in 24 hours before the payment will be removed from your account.

7. Take only the envelope of money you need for a purchase.

8. Place the receipt in the envelope after you have made that purchase.

9. What is left in the envelope is for the next time you need to buy groceries, household items, or gas. For example, on your electricity payment put what you need in your bank account, pay the bill, and if you have money left over, leave it in the envelope. This money will be used next time. You may have money left in that envelope until winter when your bills increase again. Now, you will be able to use that leftover cash you allocated based on the average amount.

10. Pay all money forward to the next month for the expense, versus spending it. If you find after three months you have money left—allocate it to savings. This does not include bills that change like energy and gas. Groceries, you might find you have started to save $100 a month on your expenses. This money can now be put into savings or spent on your credit card debt.

The idea of the "start now" budgets are to get you doing something now, so that you stop feeling anxious and like nothing is ever changing. By bolstering your confidence towards saving, you will start to enjoy what you do have and not what you cannot afford.

Furthermore, you will start having so much fun saving, you will begin to look for other ways you can start to save.

Here is one last way you can start gaining a better financial situation:

•   Go through your home.

- What have you not used for six months, not because it is a holiday decoration, but because you do not have time to use it?

- Set anything you have not used in a pile.

- Take pictures of each item.

- Sit down at your computer.

- Open a sale website like Facebook, Craigslist, eBay, etc.

- Start posting each item, with a description, image, and cost.

- Upload it, tag it, and link it with each item you have for sale.

- Repeat this process, until all items are online.

- Wait for people to see the items and contact you.

- Take that extra money and put it in savings.

If your items are not sold after two months, it is time to set up a garage sale. Host a garage sale on Friday, Saturday, and Sunday from 7am till 2pm, or until all items have been sold.

For the items that are not sold, donate them, take the deduction on your taxes.

Do not include this extra income in your budget. Forget about it. It is now in your savings. It will be used when you reach your primary goal for the first item you want.

These methods allow you not only to gain extra income, but declutter your home, as well as get your budget set up.

There are software programs you can use to design your budget. If you have trouble writing things out or starting your own budget in an excel spreadsheet, then get a budget program and start assessing your situation.

As you follow through with these methods of reducing expenses, and saving money, you will start to fall into a routine each month of adjusting your budget for your true expenses. Sometimes you may have a yearly bill, medical bill, or quarterly bill to pay, but as long as you budget for it each month, and have savings you can start to lead the life you truly wish to have.

Conclusion

Thank you again for purchasing this book!

I hope this book was able to help you with your needs and to satisfy your reading pleasures.

Now you know that how to budget your income is not hard, but it does take common sense, self-discipline, and the desire to live a debt free life. It is understandable that you might have some setbacks as you attempt to get your budget on track.

No one can change their behaviors in a day, but you can adopt a new routine, so that you stop adding to any debt you have. As soon as you put your mind to changing your mindset about how you will live and the things you truly need, you can have a better life.

Suffering comes from wanting too much and being jealous of what you don't have, instead of loving what you do have.

Use those "start now" steps to get started and prepare your budget. If you do break the budget, don't worry. Worry and stress will have you breaking that budget each month. Instead, own your faults, create a tighter budget, and work on your mindset, so that you don't go with the "I want it now," attitude you have had.

Finally, if you enjoyed this book, please take the time to share your thoughts and post a review on Amazon. It would be greatly appreciated!

Thank you and good luck!

Description

Millionaire Mind – How to Budget is going to take you through some simple, easy to start steps. Before you reach the end of this book, you will have tasks you can start immediately and start to feel comfortable about your financial situation.

You will discover how your mindset can be hindering your spending habits. You can stop letting your "want now" attitude from getting in the way, just as soon as you finish this book.

Unlike other guides available to you, this one is set up for easy reading, where you learn some real life methods for solving your debt issues, as well as getting a budget that will help you reach those goals and dreams you have.

You know there are things you wish to buy or places you want to see. It will take time. You will have to correct any debt situation you have, but rather than a lot of stories about what someone else did- you now have a guide that will take you through the steps of assessing your situation, find where you can save, and much more.

WHAT YOU WILL LEARN

- How to view your income and expenses

- Determining your recurring and non-recurring expenses

- Where you can save money and how to save that money

- How to pay off your credit card debt

Act now, so you can be debt free in a reasonable amount of time. Each person has a different amount of debt, so while someone might be debt free in a year, you may need five years.

ADDITIONAL LESSONS

1. Gain steps on changing your mindset

2. Finding new income pathways

3. How to start right this minute in creating a budget

You are ready to take the next step. You are already thinking of ways to change your spending habits for a better life—now you just need the how!

BIOGRAPHY

Christina Sorg is a passionate Money & Finance Author who creates and resides in Switzerland. Born and raised in Austria, her passion for writing and finance began early on and it has stayed with her ever since.

For three years, Christina worked abroad in Canada for a company that she founded and previously worked as an Insurance Underwriter. She quit her job at the age of 50 to pursue her writing career and take care of her family. Additionally, Christina holds a Diploma in Economics from the University of Vienna.

When she isn't writing, Christina enjoys to hike and ride her motorcycle. Most importantly, she loves spending quality time with her wonderful husband of three decades, children, and grandchildren.

Her number one mission is to educate people about the ins and outs of finance so they can stay 100% debt-free and use that money to experience the fulfilling life that they have always dreamed of.

39118561R00036

Made in the USA
Middletown, DE
05 January 2017